MARTIN
STAFFLER

VERTICAL GARDENING

MARTIN
STAFFLER

VERTICAL GARDENING

GREEN IDEAS FOR SMALL GARDENS, BALCONIES AND PATIOS

GREEN BOOKS
LONDON • OXFORD • NEW YORK • NEW DELHI • SYDNEY

Contents

PRACTICAL MATTERS

THE BASICS

- Happy Plants All Round
- Air and Root Room
- Structurally Strong – Compost
- Liquid Refreshment – Watering
- Plant Food – Fertilising
- Handle with Care!
- Overwintering
- Autumn Finale
- Pests and Diseases

HAPPY PLANTS ALL ROUND

For everything to thrive and flower in a vertical garden, you'll need to consider the requirements of your desired plants– unusual growing conditions often require unusual solutions.

As a general rule, plants can be classified according to the intensity of the sunlight they can tolerate. Some are suited to sunny flowerbeds and hot roof terraces while others thrive in shady backyards. In between, you'll find what are often called partial-shade plants and – to put it cryptically – those that flourish in shady spots. These are places sheltered from direct sun by buildings or trees, which sometimes receive more, other times less, light. For some plant varieties it is crucial that they are not exposed to strong midday sun, while others, such as lavender and Mediterranean plant species, only thrive with the maximum amount of sunshine. For most, however, a few hours of sunlight a day will be sufficient.

But don't worry! Yes, there are ideal positions for certain plants, but most will still grow in other positions if you look after them well. In fact, this can play into your hands. For example, on green walls the light intensity lessens as

> ### TIP
> On especially hot days, it is important to provide shade to plants exposed to the midday heat. A simple sunshade or awning should be sufficient for this. Otherwise, young plants in particular can quickly scorch and fail to recover.

CRANESBILL

CREEPING SPINDLE

STRAWBERRY

LADY'S MANTLE

CORAL BELLS

BERGENIA

1

2

1. Alpine strawberries need sun, and nutrient-rich soil.

2. Large planters are essential if you want to create a green wall.

you move towards the bottom of the wall. Not so much, however, that only succulents such as the houseleek and stonecrop will flourish at the top while only ferns grow at the bottom – but it can mean that salad leaves, for example, grow better at the top of the wall. You can also use shade cloth to filter out direct sunlight and protect your plants.

AIR AND ROOT ROOM

It's not only light that influences plant growth, but also temperature and ventilation.

A spot close to a sunny house wall is warmer than an exposed, draughty location. The wall both absorbs and radiates heat. Up to a certain point, this additional heat source has its advantages. But if a metal surface becomes too hot, for example, the plants in front of it will scorch.

All plants enjoy a supply of fresh air. Where air stagnates, diseases such as mildew develop and pests such as lice gather. Exposed positions on roof terraces can also stress plants.

In individual plant bags there is no competition for the roots. Hanging varieties should only be planted lower down the wall, so that they don't grow over the other plants.

STRUCTURALLY STRONG – COMPOST

When it comes to choosing compost, the same principles apply to vertical gardens as to traditional pot gardens: without good compost the plants will not take off and instead sit there looking sickly.

These days you can find a large selection of composts at local garden centres, including a range of peat-free products (if you use these, you'll also be doing your bit to counter the over-depletion of moorlands).

TIP

Even the best compost is of little benefit if you don't give the plant enough room for their roots to grow. Make sure when you're planting that the root ball doesn't touch the side of the planter and has around 1–2cm of room. The plant then has enough space to not only survive, but also develop further.

Offset guttering planted with salad leaves quickly covers a bare wall with greenery.

You can produce the right kind of soil yourself from a few ingredients, or enrich what you already have. Mix two-thirds peat-free garden soil with equal parts compost and bark humus. This mixture is particularly liked by perennials and summer flowers. For vegetables, you need to increase the compost ratio by two-thirds. If the compost consists mainly of garden waste, you can add organic fertilisers such as hoof and horn meal to balance it out. Instead of bark humus, mix in a small amount of sand. Mediterranean herbs such as lavender and thyme require fewer nutrients. With these, it makes sense to add sand and lava rock for light soils. Anyone wanting to provide succulents with the best conditions should avoid nutrient-rich garden soil. Instead, mix cactus, or potting, compost with equal parts sand, lava rock and perlite.

LIQUID REFRESHMENT – WATERING

Once you've decided on the plants for your garden, the location and the right substrate,

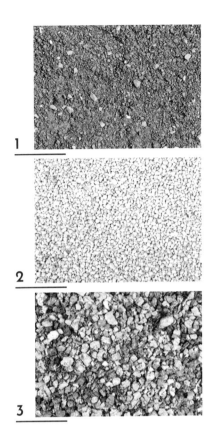

1

2

3

it's time to think about watering. You can take care of most vertical gardens manually, with a watering can for plants that are easy to access or by installing a garden hose with a watering lance for anything planted higher up. Ideally, you should never allow your plants to get too dry or cause them to sit in water. You can check moistness by dipping a finger into the compost, and only watering when the compost is drying out. After a while, you'll get a feel for when to water and by how much.

1. Gravel breaks up the soil and can be used as a drainage layer.

2. Bentonite can be worked into the soil to store water and nutrients.

3. Vermiculite improves the ability of the substrate to convey water.

1. Liquid fertiliser is added directly into the irrigation water.
2. Fertiliser pellets and sticks are simply pushed into the compost in the root area.

Over the course of the growing season, the amount you need to water will vary. On hot days it can even be necessary to water twice daily as, in contrast to plants growing in the ground, container plants cannot access water from deeper ground layers. With small containers, like tins, you can water only a little at a time, and this is quickly used up, which means going on holiday in high summer could spell disaster for your once flourishing vertical garden!

Irrigation systems

For larger projects, it's well worth thinking about installing automatic watering systems with targeted and timed droplet watering. Some suppliers offer discreet-looking, affordable systems in their range, with which plants can be watered individually. The manufacturers of green wall systems also supply watering systems tailored to the product.

PLANT FOOD – FERTILISING

Unless you've only planted professional fasters such as succulents, plants need nutrients, which are obtained from compost. If this is exhausted, they will start to wilt. With long-term fertilisers in the form of granules, pellets and sticks, you can ensure an extended food supply. The best way to deal with an acute need for nutrients is to add liquid fertiliser to the irrigation water, which takes effect immediately.

Watering systems usually consist of a thin hose that is fixed in place with pegs. Fine nozzles or holes regulate the optimal water flow.

Most plants are satisfied with complete fertilisers, which contain all the essential nutrients. Please note, blue corn fertiliser can cause nitrate poisoning, so should be avoided if you have small children or pets, or if your garden attracts lots of wildlife.

HANDLE WITH CARE!

Even though vertical gardening can be a fun and creative way to garden, having to continually maintain your green space is unavoidable – tedious as it may sometimes be when it's miserable outside.

What's the point of a perfect DIY hanging bag if it only becomes usable in September? What use is a beautiful display if it doesn't receive proper care when you're away? From the moment you plant young seedlings in May through to harvesting, you need to keep an eye on them and inspect them regularly. Are there problems with the watering? Should climber shoots be tied onto the frame? Is the fixing in the wall still stable? During the year there are various plant-specific tasks, such as pinching off the side shoots of tomatoes or pruning soft fruit bushes. An attack by pests or disease is best dealt with if detected early. And despite everything, occasionally you will have to replace plants that have died. It happens even in the best gardens.

> ### TIP
> Drawing up a schedule of regular care tasks can be really helpful. That way you can note down any particularities, such as very thirsty plants that require a smaller interval between waterings. You can also set reminders for fertilising and pruning.

STURDY WALL HANGING

ROSEMARY

DILL

STRAWBERRY

MINT

PIMPINELLA

NASTURTIUMS

BASIL

PARSLEY

'ROTE AUSLESE' PERILLA

SHISO

1. Strawberries form runners, which you can allow to root in small pots and only then detach.

2. In the autumn, prune old stems of summer raspberries to the ground.

OVERWINTERING

Vertical gardens are mostly restricted to just one season. The remains of the annuals and soil should be thrown onto the compost heap come autumn. Watering systems need to be emptied and, where necessary, stored in a frost-free environment. Equipment that is to be re-used should be thoroughly cleaned and repaired if necessary. The rest should be dismantled and correctly disposed of.

Perennials have a good chance of surviving the winter in a sheltered location. You can protect Mediterranean herbs such as lavender, rosemary and curry plant from the winter sun with permeable garden fleece or spruce bark. Many soft fruit bushes must be pruned so that they will produce fruit again the following year on freshly formed shoots, while strawberries can be salvaged for the following year via runners or dividing. It is best to plan the projects for the coming season as early as October or November. You can then acquire the equipment you need over the winter, thus having more time for assembly and planting come spring.

When autumn days grow shorter and colder, then chrysanthemums have their moment.

AUTUMN FINALE

When the salad leaves, tomatoes and remaining annuals have been completely harvested, the urban kitchen garden season is at an end. However, those with a view of their vertical projects from their living room, for example, may want to extend the green season by an additional few weeks by making a small investment. Around September and October, most garden centres supply plants for autumn planting. These tend to be specially grown ornamental leaf perennials such as coral bells (*Heuchera*) or spurge (*Euphorbia*) and small grasses, mostly sedges (*Carex*), which provide some much-needed colour during this time of the year, with their earthy autumnal tones, and structural beauty. Mini berry-bearing shrubs such as prickly heath (*Gaultheria*) provide colourful accents.

Chrysanthemums, whose colour palette ranges from white, yellow and orange through to dark red and pink, can be particularly striking. With heathers in white and pink, it's easy to achieve a cheerful colour combination, which can look rather creative when arranged vertically.

1

2

3

Low-maintenance season

Taking care of autumnal planting is a breeze. As the plants are barely growing, they require less watering and no fertiliser. This means that you can put them closer together and are thus planting the end result. Furthermore, pests and diseases are less of a concern in the autumn.

You can attempt to overwinter a few of the perennials and grasses, but they are really only intended for one season, like annuals.

1. Coral bells are herbaceous perennials with fabulous leaf colours.

2. Spurges, with their glowing autumn colouring, belong in autumn arrangements.

3. Depending on the variety, gaultheria bears red, pink or white berries.

Biological pest control: ladybirds eradicate large numbers of aphids.

Cutting off the affected parts and applying a fungicide will help to protect against fungal diseases such as powdery mildew in the short term. In the long term, the plant's location should be optimised.

PESTS AND DISEASES

Balcony and roof terrace gardens encounter far fewer unwelcome guests than in traditional gardens, where deer, rabbits and voles can cause some trouble. But for many other pests and diseases, growing height is no obstacle. To prevent lice, caterpillars and other pests, choosing the right position can make a massive difference. Pay attention to resistant strains against mildew, for example, or, in the case of tomatoes, brown rot. A nesting box for songbirds can also be helpful, so long as they take up residence: their young are famously ravenous. In just one night, snails can do a lot of damage to a vegetable plot, and while it is more difficult for pests to climb, your wall of greenery is not safe from them. Should a plague of snails threaten your precious plants, then a combination approach will help: gather by hand, make regular use of slug pellets, and be persistent.

PESTS AND DISEASES

PEST/ DISEASE	PATTERN OF DAMAGE	CAUSES	CONTROL
SNAILS	Feeding damage on vegetables and ornamental plants	Snail eggs in the compost; warm, humid weather	Slug pellets; collect
APHIDS	Sticky buds, leaves and shoots; aphids on the plants	Weakened plants; dry, warm weather	Spray off with a powerful jet of water
SPIDER MITES	Tiny insects; countless white dots on leaves, fine webs	Dry, warm weather	Regularly spray with water; use a spray treatment
CATERPILLARS	Feeding damage on leaves	Food plants of beetle larvae and caterpillars	Collect; spray with hot, soapy water; nesting boxes
BEETLES	Feeding damage on edges of leaves or holes bored in shoots	Food plants for beetles	Collect; biological control with nematodes (roundworms)
WHITEFLY	Yellow flecks on the leaves; weakened plants	Warm, humid weather	Yellow sticky fly traps
GREY MOULD	Grey coating on the leaves or fruit	Damaged and dead parts of plants and plants that are too damp	Cut off affected plant parts; use fungicide
BROWN ROT	Brown flecks on leaves and fruit	Damp, warm weather; wet leaves	Put plants under cover; plant resistant varieties; do not water the leaves
MILDEW	Powdery mildew: grey flecks on upper surface of leaf Downy mildew: grey areas on underside of leaf	With powdery mildew dry, warm weather; with downy mildew damp, warm weather, over-fertilised plants	Cut off affected plant parts; use fungicide; plant resistant varieties

Most problems can be avoided with the right location, as well as regular checks and early intervention upon discovery of a pattern of damage.

PROJECTS

GET CREATIVE!

WOODEN PALLETS

Wooden pallets, such as Euro pallets, are fantastic for vertical gardens.
Depending on requirements, you can remove boards and combine them
with items to display your plants. Simply propped up, your green
wall will be ready in no time.

PRETTY PALLETS

Vertical gardening is often associated with planting up Euro pallets. Of course, there is a lot more to it than simply standing these up and loading them with plants, but the rustic charm a humble wooden pallet provides is second to none.

Pallets were first designed to store and transport cargo – it's difficult to tell who first came up with the idea to store them upright and grow flowers in them. But the idea has spread far and wide, and is still growing in popularity.

The Euro pallet is perfect for this purpose. This is a Europe-wide standardised exchangeable pallet which, at 1200 × 800 × 144mm and around 22kg, is manageable even for novice gardeners. Check for those branded with the EPAL and EUR quality certifications (introduced in 2010), as these provide assurance that the pallets are toxin-free – an important feature when planting herbs and vegetables.

When it comes to concerns about stability, no need to worry! Euro pallet boards are held together with 78 to 81 specialised nails, so that what is usually intended for transporting up to 2,000kg on a flat surface is bound to safely support a few upright plants, together with soil and an irrigation system. The rounded edges are another plus, as they help to prevent injury.

You can order nearly new pallets via mail order and the delivery costs are often minimal despite their size. Otherwise, keep an eye on new-build estates, farms, garden centres, *etc*. With a little luck you can find used pallets in good condition for a minimal charge or even free.

QUALITY SEAL

Since 2010, Euro pallets are branded with the EPAL and EUR quality certifications.

A pallet painted in an eye-catching red and planted with grasses, fruit and low-maintenance perennials.

EYE-CATCHING DISPLAYS

Unfortunately, it is not enough to simply set a wooden pallet upright before planting it up – but there are only a few additional steps and materials required before your pallet planter will be ready. First, you need to decide which way your pallet will face. The underside provides three levels for generous planting. The upper side provides four narrow slits and a top edge for planting. Bear in mind that this also means more wood on view, so you may want to give it a colourful lick of paint.

Point of view

The underside is probably the easiest to set up since you have ready-made plant compartments via the three wooden planks, which are cut to size and screwed onto the wooden blocks from underneath. These compartments are ideal for hanging plants and those with bushy foliage, as they provide plenty of growing room.

Before planting, attach your pallet to a wall with hooks or use support feet to stand it up. To prevent the wood from rotting too quickly, you can line the bottom and sides of the compartments

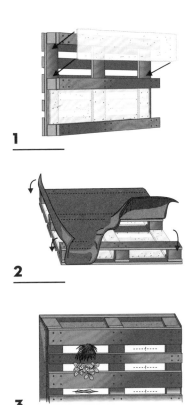

with horticultural foil. Follow this with a layer
of expanded clay, then compost. To prevent
waterlogging, drill single holes through the foil and
wooden planks. If you would like to plant up the
upper side of the pallet, attach fleece and foil to the
pallet (see diagrams). You should then select only
plants with small root balls, as you'll need to plant
them from the front through the narrow slits.

Intensive watering is required, particularly at
the outset. If you've selected plants that last all
season, you'll need to incorporate an irrigation
hose into the pallet.

1. Cut fleece to fit and
tack firmly from the
inside.

2. Firmly attach the
foil to protect the roots.
Stand the pallet up and
fill with soil.

3. Cut slits into
the fleece and insert
plants.

1

2

HANGING PALLETS

1. Gather all your equipment before you start, to make the process easier.

2. Strawberry and chilli plants can be planted in tin cans and hung on hooks.

Of course, you can't screw pallets into any wall, especially if you're renting (you'll want to get permission from your landlord before starting work). If you find you don't have space or permission to hang the larger Euro pallets, then it could be worth looking into the smaller and lighter versions, which can even be hung on balconies.

For visual reasons and to protect the wood, you'll first want to paint all surfaces of your pallet with a wood preservative. As soon as it has dried (around one to two hours), you can proceed. While you wait, you can clean the hanging baskets and tins, and get the rest of the equipment ready. You'll need: two chains of the right size/length; screws or shackles for closing the chains; hooks and screws for hanging; a screwdriver; compost; and a trowel and gloves, as well as your plants.

STRAWBERRY 'TOSCANA'

CHILI 'NASCHZIPFEL'

WINTER SAVORY 'BOLERO'

FRISÉE LETTUCE
OR CURLY ENDIVE

CHARD

CHERRY TOMATOES

CURRY PLANT 'ALADIN'

PARSLEY 'MOOSKRAUSE'

CONSTRUCTING A HANGING PALLET

A few recycled materials and well-chosen plants can be transformed into balcony shelving in no time.

1.
A simple, used wooden pallet – from bulk waste or packaging – forms the basis for this vertical gardening project.

2.

To make the wood last longer, clean it and add a coat of wood preservative or a primer and paint. If preferred, you can also sand it down beforehand.

3.
Slide a strong chain round the balustrade and pallet, and secure them with a bolt and nut.

4.
Use hanging flowerpots or cleaned food tins as plant containers by simply attaching the half-open lids over screwed-in hooks, or drill a hole in the tins and screw on.

5.

Fill with plant compost, but be sure to leave room for the root balls. If possible, drill a drainage hole and add a thin drainage layer.

6.
Add plants, such as strawberries. Make sure to leave enough space around the edge of the container so that you can easily water them. Small containers will require frequent watering, but please be careful to avoid waterlogging.

Gaps can have a visually disruptive effect. They can be easily covered by hanging up a decorative item, or you could hang up a pair of scissors, for harvesting produce, or a small watering can.

It is difficult to estimate which plants will fit securely into which container, and how many containers you'll be able to fit on the pallet. If possible, you should buy more than you're likely to need. Ideally, fill the larger pots first with a few peppers and tomatoes, as well as curry plant and basil. Then place salad leaves in the smaller containers, since these are available as young plants, often in trays of six or twelve. That way you'll have the cheaper, young plants leftover at the end, which you can then plant elsewhere without difficulty. You'll find a small watering can is useful for accurate and carefully dosed watering. It's also a good idea to thoroughly soak the plants in a bucket of water in advance of planting by dunking them in their plastic pots until the air bubbles disappear.

Arranging a variety

Now you can carefully mount the pallets on the balcony balustrade using the chains. Ask someone to help you lift them into place, or sit them temporarily on a stool of the right height. If necessary, protect the railing by placing pieces of wood or leather underneath the chains. Then you can finally get going with arranging and planting up your containers. As you do this, remember to bear in mind how big the plants will grow and whether they are bushy or hanging varieties. Sun-hungry plants should be placed higher up if possible.

An elegant, chic grey wall screen with yellow-green hanging plants.

PRIVACY SCREENS

While planted up pallets make fantastic shelves, they can also function as practical and pretty privacy screens or for blocking unpleasant draughts. For these, constructing stable footing is crucial. On patios and balconies, for example, you can only really work with floor stands. One method is to place the upright pallet onto two beams laid on the ground, then mount these with four diagonal battens. Don't scrimp on the length and thickness of the beams as they need to counterbalance the force of the wind on the pallet. The beams should have at least a 10cm edge and protrude beyond the pallet for 50cm. Anchoring the pallet to the wall and ceiling with a wire cable will provide extra security.

Stability

If desired, for example at the edge of the patio, you can try a more modern style. Drive two sinkable steel ground sockets, also called

metposts, into the ground at a distance of about 80cm. Now push two wooden posts of matching lengths with a maximum 7.5cm edge into the steel sockets. By preventing contact with the soil, you'll delay any potential rotting. Now slip the pallet over the vertical wooden posts and it will stand securely. If you cannot lift the pallet up that high, first place it on the two ground sockets, secure it and then feed the posts through from the top. If necessary, you can then screw the pallet to the posts.

1. Ground sockets and wooden posts help to support the pallets.

2. Saw off heavily damaged parts.

3. Preparatory work: sand down and then varnish.

1. Knock two metposts into the ground with a sledgehammer.
2. Then place the posts through the underside of the pallet into the metposts.

If the posts are long enough you can then mount two pallets, one on top of the other, creating a taller privacy screen. It is also possible to go midway, by sawing one of the pallets in two to your desired height. Depending on what you want, you can plant up part of the pallet to allow views through the gaps, or completely plant it up for full privacy.

Garden furniture

If you have ground-space for more projects, why not create matching garden furniture from the pallets, such as a table and chairs. The easiest method is to stack several pallets until you get the desired height for your table, then fix together using a hollow punch. For the chairs, assemble from stacked pallets and add further pallets to the sides and back as arm- and backrests, before firmly screwing together using a hollow punch.

Better screening and a more colourful display can be achieved with bright hanging pots full of summer flowers. If posts are long enough, you can even mount two pallets on top of each other to create taller screening.

Food storage containers are great for planting up the top edge of your pallets.

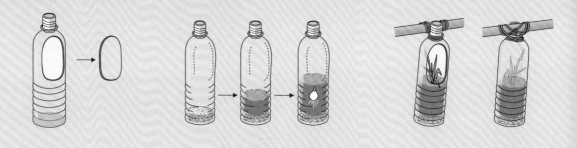

BOTTLE GREENHOUSE

Using a Stanley knife, cut a large hole in the top part of an empty recyclable bottle. Then pour in a thin layer of gravel, followed by some soil. Place spring bulbs through the opening and cover with soil. Hang up the bottles and water regularly.

CREATIVE RECYCLING

Thankfully, more and more people today are shunning mass consumerism and throw-away culture in favour of reusing and recycling. Not only is it more economical, but it's also an easy way to help the planet.

If you haven't already noticed, recycling is a major part of vertical gardening! Whether on a large scale with pallets, or smaller scale with tins and bottles, we are continually endeavouring to get one further use out of our waste. Look around you and you'll find numerous possibilities for recycled plant containers. For this to be successful, it's helpful to get acquainted with the requirements of your plants: hanging plants have a different space requirement to shrubs; Mediterranean herbs tolerate more dryness than classic kitchen herbs, while some vegetables, such as courgettes, require so much water that larger bags and tubs are necessary to meet their needs.

BOTTLE PARTY

Most glass and recyclable bottles are reused several times, or are at least recycled on a large scale. But even single-use plastic bottles can be transformed into fun features for the garden.

For your kitchen or balcony, why not try planting spring onions in bottles and hanging them along a pole? The bottles provide the perfect growing conditions for spring onions as they're warm and humid but the bottle openings give a continual air supply. The green stalks that grow out of the top are also a pretty sight!

SPRING ONIONS

Spring onions are milder than cooking onions, making them perfect for salads.

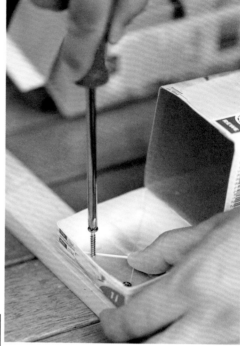

DRINKS CARTONS

The range of materials in most drinks cartons makes recycling them far from simple. This makes repurposing empty cartons as a temporary home for your plants before disposing of them even more appealing. Due to weathering, watering and soil, they will be looking tired at the end of the season, but there is bound to be a fresh supply next year. As with most recycling projects, repeated patterns and rows look better than a mishmash of individual pieces.

And while plastic bottles are a more long-lasting plant container, drinks cartons, with their colourful designs, can be more visually striking in a vertical garden.

Watering tip

Due to the short lifespan of cartons outdoors, they are better used as containers for herbs and vegetables. However, do take care when watering; use your finger to feel the soil in each container to see how dry it is before drenching the soil.

1. After cleaning the drinks carton, cut the base on three sides with a Stanley knife and fold down.

2. Add two small screws to the carton lid, then attach your new plant container to a wooden batten or directly to a wall.

THYME

PARSLEY AND CHIVES

WATER LETTUCE

SILVER THYME

HOUSELEEK AND STONECROP

WINTER SAVORY

HOUSELEEK

BASIL

ALPINE STRAWBERRY

1. The holes in a colander prevent your plants from getting waterlogged; line with newspaper first to prevent the soil trickling out.

2. You can arrange tea lights for decoration in stainless steel pan scrubbers.

MOVEABLE SHELVES

Often ladders stand around unused throughout the year in the garage or shed, making them ideal as movable shelves. Step ladders and small steps are perfectly suited for freestanding, vertical scaffolds. Ladders are no less decorative when propped against a wall. Now it's just a matter of assembling the right selection of plant containers. For content and visual effect, spare pots and pans, colanders, bowls, baking tins, beakers and other kitchen utensils are an excellent choice.

Stainless steel and cast iron utensils are very weather-resistant, making them the most suitable for garden decoration. Old and robust objects in enamel also look very elegant. Plastic containers usually do not keep as long and easily become brittle, but they should last for at least a season.

Water fans take note: you can even create a mini-pond, as in this measuring jug populated with water lettuce (*Pistia*).

1,001 IDEAS

There are limitless possibilities for repurposing everyday objects for the garden that would otherwise be discarded in your attic. While some items might give up the ghost after just a few weeks – or even days – others, by contrast, will go on for several years.

The remains of an old gutter, for example, can be converted into a new generation balcony planter. With a few simple steps, you can install it on several levels on a specially constructed wooden framework. Salad leaves do not need a lot of soil to thrive, so you can use them to plant up the gutter lengths.

Kitchen pot pourri

Some plants work well when placed on the steps of the ladder in containers, while others are better suited for hanging up. In this way, you can quickly populate a colourful collection with suitable plants. However, do bear in mind that some kitchen items have their shortcomings. For example, it is difficult to drill drainage holes for excess water into the base of steel and cast iron pots and pans. For these, your best bet is to set the containers under a roofed location, such as a balcony, where you regulate watering better than out in the open air, where waterlogging will inevitably occur. A soup ladle hanging up provides ample room for houseleeks, and a measuring jug can serve as a mini-pond.

FOLDABLE SHELVES

One of the quickest and most flexible vertical planting installations is a simple ladder.

1.
A quick rummage through your cupboards can reveal a load of unused containers, providing you with lots of options when you plant – and less clutter!

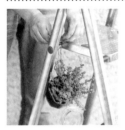

2.
Preserve jars with a handle are well suited for both sitting on a ladder and hanging up. Keep the rubber seal for later use.

3.
Smaller containers, such as egg cups, are perfect for succulents and other small plants. Use them to visually plug small gaps on the steps.

4.
Placed individually, or elegantly situated next to each other, these old pots radiate a harmonious unity.

5.
Even soup ladles, hung up and filled with a little light substrate for succulents, can make for a stylish container.

6.
Should something not work out, don't worry! Here, a dustpan has been planted up, but there's another spare one for use in the kitchen!

Plastic planters decorated with crocheted yarn look lovely when attached to a house wall as hanging shelves. Make sure to use hardwearing yarn, cord or rope, so that the shelf does not break due to the weight or sink after being watered.

A washing line with particular charm – a sense of humour is always welcome when it comes to vertical gardening!

1. Row by row, in several gutters, salad leaves can be harvested throughout the summer.
2. Two containers made from a single recyclable bottle, which can be hung by chains one above the other in a column.

If you only have a narrow area for hanging containers, one solution is to cut recyclable bottles in half and arrange them one on top of the other on chains. For small bottles you should be able to attach the run of chains on both sides of the bottle with safety pins. Larger bottles with more weight should be fixed to the chain with screws. Hanging herbs, such as trailing rosemary, look especially beautiful with these. Kitchen herbs like parsley, chives and basil can be easily grown from seed, and young sage, rocket and lettuce plants also work well.

Discarded

There's even a spot for underwear from your granny's old trunk on the washing line in the vertical garden! All you need to do is sew the openings of pants and vests so that the soil stays in place. Instead of customary clothes pegs, sturdy hooks and chains are advisable. Old jeans, with the legs sewn up, make great planters. Even old handbags, attached to a wall, can be used for a collection of hanging plants. If you're a knitter or a crocheter, line small pots with foil then create colourful pot covers for your new planters. With a bit of imagination, the sky's the limit!

IT'S THAT EASY

With just a piece of tarpaulin (60 x 185cm) as well as a section of cord or rope (at least 250cm in length) threaded to form a U shape, you can make a roomy strawberry bag with this sewing pattern.

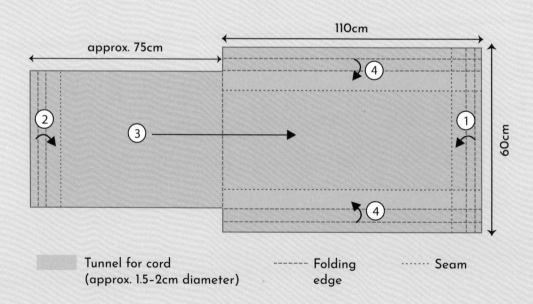

Tunnel for cord
(approx. 1.5-2cm diameter)

----- Folding edge

.... Seam

BAG GARDENING

While bags generally don't have a lot in common with flowerpots, both are easy to fill. The soft outer skin of a bag ensures a more informal look, which is in tune with the rustic feel of a vertical garden.

For a long time now, modern urban gardeners have been discovering the advantages of planted-up bags. They are lighter in their unplanted state and more space-saving than conventional pots, and they also create visual interest. Potatoes and salad items planted directly into growbags in the garden can thrive for a really long time, and large bags and hessian sacks planted with pumpkins and strawberries can even be placed in a wall niche or on a roof terrace. When hung up, handles make bags of greenery look especially distinguished against plant pots.

SELECTING THE RIGHT BAGS

As with containers, take stock of what you have spare or lying around the house, or you can make a suitable model yourself. While you can find decorative bags online or through any good garden centre, most do-it-yourself gardeners will have a go at making their own bags.

Material remnants are perfect for sewing, while plastic sheets can be glued. Where possible, bags that are able to immediately take several plants are especially useful, like the strawberry bag on the next page. In the front there is room for up to eight little plants. As a practical hanging solution, a rope threaded through works well as it also gives the bag stability. If you opt for a robust plastic sheet, it's possible you'll be able to reuse it the following year.

CONTINUOUS CROPPING

Ideal for bag gardening: the Alpine strawberry 'Rügen', with its small, delicious berries.

DIY STRAWBERRY BAG

Follow the instructions below to make your bag, and in no time at all, you can get on with planting!

1.

Using a sharp knife, cut six or eight cross-shaped slits into the front of the bag you have sewed.

2.

Now carefully fill the bag with soil (pre-fertilised soil is best here).

3.

Carefully wrap the fragile young shoots in aluminium foil, so that a small point forms at the top.

4.

Push the foil-covered plants through the slits from the inside, before removing the foil.

5.

Until the plants are better established, it's sensible to water the little individual plants with the aid of a funnel.

6.

For the first two weeks, leave the strawberry bag lying down with the top folded over and closed. Then hang the bag up on the cord.

Depending on the strawberry variety, you can start harvesting the delicious fruit as early as June and continue to do so throughout the summer.

Location issues

When it comes to planting strawberries or other crops, choosing the right compost is crucial. For a successful supply of fresh produce, the soil should be rich in nutrients – pre-fertilised. Alternatively, you can work in your own, well-rotted compost and occasionally add additional fertiliser over the course of the season. Using liquid fertiliser when watering ensures quick results, while continuous-release plant food in the form of pellets or sticks releases nutrients little by little. A sunny, but not scorching, location is ideal. The hotter it is, the more you have to water – although do bear in mind that in cool, shady places the harvest will naturally be smaller.

BURLAP HERB SACKS

You can get a comparable number of herb plants to those in the strawberry bag by mounting small burlap bags in a column. Three to four such sacks can be tied together with a rope without a problem, and then attached to a wall. Depending on the size of the burlap sacks, you'll be able to fit one or two herb plants. Line the sacks with foil or freezer bags to prevent soil seeping out. You could sew the sacks yourself if you'd prefer, otherwise you should be able to source ready-made

1

2

1. First fill the bags with some compost.

2. Then remove the herbs from their pots and gently push the root balls into the compost.

ones. Look for models that already have metal eyelets for closing the sacks. The rope can be easily threaded through these and fixed in place with a knot. Secure with additional stitching to prevent tearing to holes cut into the burlap.

PRE-MADE BAGS

For those less gifted in handicrafts, but who nevertheless would like to pep up a shabby railing or wall with a plant bag, there are plenty of pre-made bag styles to choose from. You'll find something to fit whatever space you have available for hanging up, screwing on or simply hanging over, for both inside and outside, for house walls, sheds or the washing line, for the balcony or a roof terrace. More sophisticated bags, like Verti-Plant®, have built-in watering systems with drainage holes in the top two bags, allowing water to drain to the one below while the bottom one is impermeable to prevent water leaking onto your balcony. You can easily transfer this method to one of your own creations using several levels of plants.

It's important to water the right amount. The plants should not completely dry out, but also should never be swamped or made to sit in standing water. Small holes in the bottom of the bag will allow excess water to run off.

Hang your bags close to the kitchen and you will always have the herbs in view, making it easier and more convenient to harvest them.

MINT

FRENCH LAVENDER

PURPLE SAGE
'PURPURASCENS'

THYME

STRAWBERRY

OREGANO

WINTER SAVORY

2

1

1. Saddle up! With a saddle bag you can embellish both sides of a balcony railing.

2. Verti-Plant® from Burgon & Ball (see page 90) for six plants can quickly be installed on any wooden fence.

For gardeners who are fed up with their balcony flowers hanging on the outside, facing the street below, rather than into their own balcony, a saddlebag that is plantable on both sides is the perfect solution. They also don't need any additional fixing.

You can even make your own version with a rope and two bags of equal size. Knot the bags together and hang as desired over the railing, fill with compost and plant up on both sides so that everyone gets to enjoy the sumptuous flowers.

LIVING PLANT MURALS

Some people see them as a gimmick, while others appreciate the practical benefit. Either way, there is no doubt about it – living plant murals are gaining in popularity. Think of them as your own mini version of a green wall, or a modern green façade!

CONSTRUCTING A LIVING PLANT MURAL

Indoor and outdoor living plant murals are striking additions to the garden. Furthermore, these are easy to care for and look really elegant.

1.
First, remove the protective film from the front of the square.

2.
You'll see cross-shaped slits in the fleece. Open these up carefully - specialised substrate lies underneath.

3.
Young plants (< 9cm), such as Bird's Nest Fern (*Asplenium nidus*), do not have root balls and can easily be placed into the mini-bags.

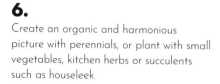

4.
You can hang the square frame like a normal picture. Align the frame with a spirit level and mark drill holes.

5.
Hang according to the instructions and water via the opening on the top. Custom watering systems are often also available for these.

6.
Create an organic and harmonious picture with perennials, or plant with small vegetables, kitchen herbs or succulents such as houseleek.

Low-maintenance houseleeks are perfect candidates for living plant murals. They love dryness and sunlight.

Just like the other planter projects in this section, the interplay of substrate, plant, lighting and watering is crucial for living plant murals to flourish. You don't have to make everything yourself – there's a variety ready-made products on the market (see page 90). Following initial teething difficulties, these models are gaining in popularity. However, keep in mind that even with all due care, you won't avoid having to replace individual plants or undertaking a completely new planting at the start of the season.

Watering

All living plant murals follow the same principle: specialised plant compost is concealed behind a fleece or foil sheet, which is held in a frame. You then insert your plants as desired through the slits in the sheet. For these to take root, the root balls should be well watered beforehand and the compost should also be dampened. For best results, let the whole thing start to grow while lying flat and only hang up the mural after two or three weeks. This prevents the soil trickling out, or plants from falling out before stronger roots have formed. The sunnier the location, the more often you have to water. An automatic watering system in the form of drip irrigation is best. Those who enjoy DIY can easily construct such a mural from a few slats, a fleece and a flat board for the back.

HANGING PLANTS AND CLIMBERS

For anyone wanting an unusual addition to their vertical garden, why not try spherical kokedamas (moss balls) or hanging tomato plants?

Kokedamas originated in Japan. There, small bonsais are grown in moss balls. Numerous other plants can also be cultivated in this way, including bulbs such as narcissi and hyacinths, succulents such as houseleek and echeverias, and orchids such as butterfly orchids. Kokedamas can be arranged in hanging formations, as they are in Japan, but you can also place them on decorative dishes.

There are also several options for making the spheres. Mix damp, clay-based soil with peat and shape a sphere out of it. Drill a hole in it, into which the plant is placed. Then wrap the whole thing in pieces of moss, held in place with thin florist's wire or crafting wire.

This is a particularly good way to introduce plants without root balls, such as flower bulbs or single-growing shoots. For indoor orchids,

TIP

In vertical gardens that mainly contain rustic recycling ideas, moss balls may seem rather out of place. However, you don't have to miss out! Instead, cut open tennis or juggling balls and plant them up just like traditional kokedamas.

Indoor orchids, such as phalaenopsis varieties, look especially elegant in kokedamas, as the flower shoots tend to hang downwards, making for a unique display.

be sure to use loose orchid substrate rather than clay-based soil for your kokedamas. The moss will help you to mould it into a more or less spherical shape.

You can also use floral foam, purchased from most garden centres or craft shops. Shape a 'moss ball' by adding soil around the foam, then covering in moss. Bore holes into this with wire and sink the cuttings into them.

Looking after kokedamas is really easy. For most plants it is enough to simply spray them with water. The spheres also cope really well with an occasional soaking in a bath. However, don't forget to let them drain before hanging back up. You can also add liquid fertiliser to the water when watering.

HANGING TOMATOES

Dyed-in-the-wool kitchen gardeners will protest, but the idea of cultivating hanging tomatoes is so good perhaps because of how unconventional it is! With the advent of the 'Topsy Turvy' tomato variety and hanging growbags, this innovative technique for growing tomatoes is quickly becoming more popular. For a true DIY approach, drill a hole into the base of a plastic bucket with handles, fill the bucket with soil, plant the young tomato plant and hang up. There are several advantages to this system: you no longer need a tomato bed with canes, and snails can't get to your tomatoes!

HOW TO MAKE A KOKEDAMA

Add a touch of floristry to your balcony with this elegant planting method from Japan.

1.
You'll need a moss cushion, string, some soil and drought-loving succulents such as echeverias.

2.
Remove the plants from their pots and carefully round off the root. If the root balls are very small, add some damp earth material.

3.
Spread out the moss cushion with the soil side facing up and position the plant in the centre.

4.
Now carefully fold the moss up and over the root ball, making a sphere. When you're happy with the shape, use the string to firmly tie from all sides.

5.
Dunk the moss sphere in water for as long as it takes for it to become saturated. Then allow to drain.

6.
Cut string to the desired length and hang up the kokedama like a mobile, or attach to cut twigs.

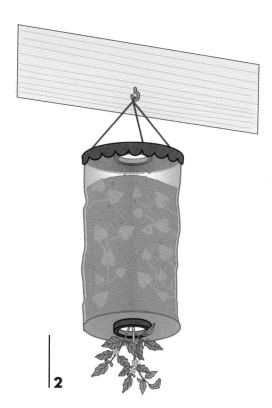

1. Small plants are placed in the special holder upside down through the hole in the base.

2. Filled with soil, the whole thing is hung from the ceiling or a suitable stand.

The tomato container can also be hung up if desired, so long as the fixing is sturdy enough to hold the weight, which is considerable once you've filled it with soil and watered the plants. You need really sturdy ceilings for a hook or a suitable rod for hanging on. It's also worth bearing in mind that the higher the plants hang, the more effort it will take to water them. A step ladder works as a quick solution, although an automatic watering system is better. If you're hanging the tomato plant in the open air, then it will, like the conventional varieties, be susceptible to brown rot. Resistant strains are a good solution. The plants grow both upwards and downwards. Cherry tomatoes are preferable over plants with larger fruits because they weigh less.

Space-saving: climbing vegetable varieties grow up cables or trellises on the wall.

A roofed location is ideal for these tomato plants in a raised bed as it helps prevent brown rot. The ensemble is completed by wooden crates planted with lettuces and other vegetables.

CLIMBERS

When grown on cords, climbing plants such as tomatoes, cucumbers or pumpkins, make for a fantastic display, at once both traditional and chic. To do this you'll need to mount two brackets on a wall and link them with a crossbar. Place a small bed or raised bed underneath. Then, attach the right number of cords for your plants between the two brackets. Do not underestimate the vigorous growth of the plants when you do this; you'll fit around two to three plants per metre. Depending on the varieties planted, you should use 1.5–3m of cord per plant. Once planted, carefully guide the growing shoots of the young plants onto the cords and attach. Repeat this occasionally throughout the growing season. If needed, you can tie on the heavier fruits in order to relieve the plants of the weight. Note, tomatoes, cucumbers and pumpkins are all very thirsty and greedy for fertiliser.

RAMBLING PLANTS

TYPE	PLANT HEIGHT	USE	APPEARANCE
TOMATO	100 – 250cm	Edible, harvest some from June, most from August	Red, yellow and striped varieties, round, oval or elongated
CUCUMBER	Up to 250cm	Edible, harvest from June	Green or yellow varieties
PUMPKIN	150 – 200cm	Edible, harvest from September	Round or elongated fruits
RUNNER BEANS	200 – 300cm	Edible, from July	Elongated pods
PEAS	60 – 100cm	Edible, harvest from June	Elongated pods
SWEET PEA	Up to 150cm	Decorative, annual	White, pink or violet flowers (Jun–Oct)
BLACK-EYED SUSAN	Up to 200cm	Decorative, annual	Yellow or orange-coloured flowers (Jul–Oct)
MORNING GLORY	200 – 300cm	Decorative, annual	Blue or violet flowers (Jun–Oct), mainly blooms in the morning
NASTURTIUM	Up to 100cm	Decorative, annual, edible seeds and flowers	Yellow or orange-coloured flowers (Jul–Oct), decorative leaves
HONEYSUCKLE	200 – 300cm	Decorative, perennial	Orange-red or white-pink flowers (Jun–Oct)
PURPLE BELL VINE	Up to 150cm	Decorative, annual	Violet-pink or white flowers (Jul–Oct)

You can easily influence the height of rambling plants with a trellis or, if growth is too vigorous, intervention with secateurs. Provide assistance initially by guiding the shoots onto the trellis.

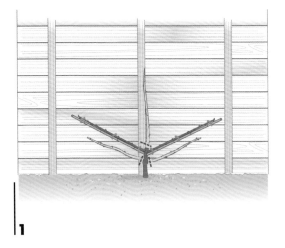
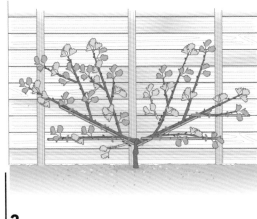

1. Shortening the main shoot after planting in the autumn promotes branching out.

2. Tie side shoots laterally to battens, first of all at a 45° angle, and then in the second year at a 90° angle.

ESPALIER FRUIT TREES

Most of the vertical gardening methods in this book are temporary and provide room every year for new ideas and opportunities to plant with vegetables, summer flowers and herbs. It makes sense, though, to have a combination of these with some projects spanning several years, thus ensuring a consistent backdrop. Espalier fruit trees are good for greening walls and simultaneously expanding the range of crops. Varieties that remain small, like gooseberry, red currant or peach, fit on patios and balconies. Anyone wanting to make a larger wall look green long-term is well-advised to choose apples and pears. However, the espaliered fruit plants that nurseries tend to stock can be costly.

Berries

Raspberries and blackberries can easily be trained into an espalier, since they produce fresh canes each year, so every year you'll need to train the shoots afresh into a fan shape. Other berry plants require patience and a bit more know-how. The main thing is to start off from a low stem – for a gooseberry plant, for example, prune the main shoot and two or three side shoots consistently, and purposefully guide the shoots over several years.

Remove excess side shoots so that the growth is more diagonally outwards rather than inwards. Every two to three years, remove the older shoots and make room for new shoots, which produce more fruit.

Starting off with two shoots from the base, in the second year the gooseberry plant forms a slightly fanned espalier.

CONSTRUCTING A GABION

Gardeners with very little or even no experience can successfully construct a gabion using ready-made elements and irregular material.

1.
You will need wire elements for assembling and stones for filling the resulting wire baskets, as well as plants, soil and gravel to cover.

2.
Pay particular attention to the side-on view, selecting the best-looking stones. Then layer up the inner filling material as you like.

3.
Mix together soil, sand and gravel into a permeable substrate. By doing this you are creating good growing conditions for the plants.

4.
In the spots where plants are to be inserted, add some substrate between the stones and push the well-watered plants in through the wire mesh.

5.
Fill the top with a layer of substrate, in which you place more plants. Add a covering of gravel or crushed stone to finish off, to make it look more attractive.

6.
Gabions can easily be stacked on top of each other or set next to one another to make any shape. They're also ideal when used as screening or to retain a slope.

For succulents and rockery plants to thrive, water less and ensure good drainage. A sunny place is ideal.

DRYSTONE WALL 2.0 – GABIONS

The perfect marriage of traditional and modern design can be achieved through planted-up wire cages, also known as gabions. Although they are becoming more common in gardens, gabions very rarely work well in traditional gardens, where they often feel inappropriate because they don't coordinate with other concepts in the garden. In contrast, in vertical gardens, with their many recycled and DIY installations, gabions fit in brilliantly as a wall or mini-tower. The principle is extremely simple. Fill ready-made wire mesh cages with natural stones or recycled material, such as bricks, and add plants. Due to the heavy weight involved, you should find out the exact potential load-bearing capacity of roof terraces or balconies, and in every case determine the position for the gabion in advance. Pushing them into a new position later is impossible.

Rockery

Just like dry stone walls, gabions look best planted up and yet can still appear natural. During the construction phase, you should already be inserting drought-loving succulents, such as houseleeks and stonecrop, in a loose arrangement, as well as rockery plants like aubretia, which overhangs decoratively and flowers in the spring. The tops of the gabions provide an opportunity for additional plants to be grown.

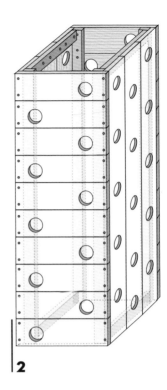

'SWISS CHEESE' PLANTER

1. Cut holes that are at least 7cm in diameter into the planks with a hole saw. Use an old plank as a base when you do this.

2. Screw the planks with holes vertically to a framework of square timbers. To provide even more stability, screw diagonal battens on the inside.

Four lengths of squared-off timber and a larger number of planks can be screwed together to make a conventional raised bed. But for those with very little ground area available, it's better to modify the idea of a raised bed to suit your space.

To do this, take longer timbers and saw the planks into shorter pieces. With this you can erect a mini wooden tower. This is where the fun part comes in – in order to create a planting area of similar size to a conventional raised bed, use a hole saw (drill attachment) to cut out circles around the tower. In addition to the plantable top surface, you can populate these holes with small strawberry plants, salad leaves and herbs. On the very top, go for larger varieties, such as borage, marigolds or mints. To make it more stable, sink the timbers 30–50cm into the ground.

KEY

☀ Full sun

⛅ Partial-shade

☁ Shade

💧 Watering required

🌸 Fertilising required

Annual

Perennial

Fragrant

Pruning required

Climbing plant

PLANTS FOR VERTICAL GARDENS

CORAL BELLS
— *Heucheras*

APPEARANCE Bushy growth. Pink, coral or white blossom in June and July. Green, brown-red, orange-red, silver-green or yellow-green decorative leaves.

CARE Really easy plants to care for.

VARIETIES Many kinds available such as 'Cappuccino', which has purple-chestnut brown leaves or 'Frosted Violet' with pink-violet leaf colouring and silvery sprinkles that turn to a bronze-violet in summer.

LOCATION Do not plant in really hot locations.

SEA THRIFT
— *Armeria maritima*

APPEARANCE Sea thrifts are enchanting with their carnation-like pink or white flowers in May and June. They have blue-green, glasslike foliage.

CARE You should deadhead after flowering. These plants require little watering.

VARIETIES The 'Alba' variety has white flowers, 'Düsseldorfer Stolz' pink ones.

LOCATION Without fail on permeable substrate, and take care to provide good drainage. Sea thrift is suitable for small planters.

AUBRIETA
— *Aubrieta* hybrids

APPEARANCE Aubrieta blooms extravagantly as early as April and May in violet-blue or white. It produces blankets of flowers that drape attractively.

CARE Once they have flowered, these should be revitalised by pruning. Apart from that, these plants are easy to care for.

VARIETIES The variety 'Blaumeise' blooms in a magnificent blue, 'Winterling' pure white. This photo shows the 'Bob Sanders' variety.

LOCATION Ensure permeable substrate and good drainage. Aubrieta looks fabulous in gabions or hanging containers.

DALMATION BELLFLOWER

— *Campanula portenschlagiana*

APPEARANCE From June to August bears wonderful blue star-shaped flowers. Blanket growth with hanging tendrils.

CARE The plants are very undemanding.

VARIETIES 'Birch' is a blue, well-known variety. The Serbian Bellflower (*Campanula poscharskyana*) is similar. A beautiful white variety is 'Silver Rain'. It trails even more than the Dalmation Bellflower.

LOCATION Tends to be rampant and therefore should not be planted with weaker growing kinds in a container.

YELLOW CORYDALIS

— *Pseudofumaria lutea*

APPEARANCE Blooms from May to October with delicate yellow flowers. Its filigree leaves are also very decorative once the flowering period is over. Bushy in growth, slightly hanging.

CARE Apart from occasional watering, no further care is necessary.

VARIETIES Pale Corydalis (*Pseudofumaria alba*). Has similar requirements, but its flowers are white-green.

LOCATION Grows in sunny to shady locations in wall cracks, gabions and small pots. Self-seeding in favourable locations.

PINKS

— *Dianthus* varieties

APPEARANCE Flower from May to August in pink and white.

CARE Low maintenance, doesn't need fertiliser and only needs watering occasionally.

VARIETIES Cheddar pinks are especially good in pot gardens (*Dianthus gratianopolitanus*, see photo) and the Clove pinks (*D. plumarius*).

LOCATION Ensure permeable substrate and drainage. These dainty ground cover perennials are particularly good for small planters, on the tops of walls and similar locations.

BUGLE
— *Ajuga reptans*

APPEARANCE Violet, white or pink flowers in May and June, shallow-growing perennial with decorative foliage.

CARE Ajuga is very undemanding and should only be watered occasionally. Vigorous growth, so do not combine with other less rapid growing perennials in one container.

VARIETIES The red-leaved dark purple bugle (*A. reptans* 'Atropurpurea') has decorative red-brown leaves. The 'Sanne' variety has white flowers, 'Tottenham' pink ones.

LOCATION Bugle prefers to be in partial-shade and slightly damp.

CRANESBILL
— *Geranium* varieties

APPEARANCE Cranesbills are perennials with decorative foliage and attractive blossoms in white, pink or blue-violet. They flower as a rule from May 10 July, some into October.

CARE Robust plants that, apart from an occasional watering, require little attention.

VARIETIES For containers, bear in mind varieties that stay small such as the Ashy Cranesbill (*G. cinereum*), the Caucasus Cranesbill (*G. renardii*) or Dwarf Garden Cranesbill (*G. cultorum* 'Tanya Rendall', see photo).

HOSTA
— *Hosta* varieties

APPEARANCE Decorative foliage plants with strikingly big leaves in light green, blue green or yellow-green. White and yellow varieties are particularly eye-catching. The flowers are on top of long stalks.

CARE In early spring protect against snails (slug pellets!). They only need a little watering.

VARIETIES A mind-bogglingly wide range. Best for small containers are varieties that remain small such as 'Abby' and 'Little Jay'.

LOCATION The ideal candidate for giving a boost to dark corners.

GRASSES

— Varieties that remain small

APPEARANCE Bushy and fluffy grass tufts with decorative panicles. The dried stalks provide an ornamental effect in winter as well.

CARE An easy-to-care-for group of plants. Only prune in early spring before new growth starts.

VARIETIES Small sedge varieties such as Blue Fescue (*Festuca cinerea*) in sun, Hair Sedge (*Carex comans*, 'Frosted Curls', see photo) in sun and partial-shade, Great Wood-rush (*Luzula sylvatica*) for shady locations.

LOCATION Ideal for use as elegant gap-fillers.

FERNS

— Varieties that remain small

APPEARANCE Decorative, fresh green fern fronds enrich darker areas of the vertical garden.

CARE Easy-care plants that like it rather damp. Cut off old fern fronds in the spring.

VARIETIES Maidenhair Spleenwort (*Asplenium trichomanes*) for small wall cracks, Deer Fern (*Blechnum spicant*) in larger containers. Hart's-tongue Fern (*Phyllitis scolopendrium*) has flat fronds.

LOCATION Ferns love damp fresh air; the substrate can be damp and rich in humus.

TUFTED PHLOX

— *Phlox* varieties

APPEARANCE Tufted Phlox (*Phlox douglasii*) is a low-growing plant that flowers abundantly from May to June in white, pink or violet.

CARE These are robust spring bloomers which, apart from infrequent watering, require little attention.

VARIETIES Tufted Phlox has fabulous varieties, such as 'Lilac Cloud' with its soft pink blossom and *P. subulata* 'Red Wings' in a vibrant light red with a magenta eye (see photo). Wild Blue Phlox (*P. divaricata*) 'Clouds of Perfume' has violet-blue flowers.

LOCATION Tolerates occasional drought.

STONECROP

—— *Sedum varieties*

APPEARANCE Carpet-forming. White, pink or yellow flowers in June and July.

CARE Apart from infrequent light watering, no further care is required.

VARIETIES Orange Stonecrop (*Sedum floriferum*) 'Weihenstephaner Gold' has glowing yellow flowers and thrives both in sunny and partial-shaded positions. The yellow-flowering Goldmoss Stonecrop (*S. acre*) prefers direct sunlight. The Caucasian Stonecrop (*S. spurium*) grows in sunny and partial-shaded positions.

LOCATION Plant in permeable substrate. Suitable for small spaces.

HOUSELEEKS

—— *Sempervivum varieties*

APPEARANCE Houseleeks are plants with ornamental leaves that form rosettes, which are usually green, red-brown or pink but come in numerous colour variants. Their flowers are pink.

CARE Minimal care is required; water very infrequently.

VARIETIES There are many hybrids and varieties with decorative leaves such as the brown-red variety 'Bronze Pastel' and the hybrid 'Rubin' in red-green.

LOCATION Always plant in permeable succulent substrate. Stonecrop is suitable for the smallest of niches.

ALOE

—— *Aloe vera*

APPEARANCE The aloe bears sharp lancet-like leaves. It occasionally produces yellow-orange flowers.

CARE The ideal plant for lazy gardeners, as it can go for weeks without being watered. Overwinter in a light and warm place indoors. Aloes can keep well as indoor plants all year round.

VARIETIES The Candelabra or Torch Aloe (*Aloe arborescens*) has branching growth.

LOCATION Must be planted in permeable succulent substrate. Note, aloe is well suited to being a kokedama plant.

ECHEVERIA

— *Echeveria varieties*

APPEARANCE The leaf rosettes of echeverias are similar to those of houseleek, but the yellow-orange flower is even more striking.

CARE Echeverias only have to be watered infrequently. Too much water will quickly cause rot to set in. The plants are best overwintered indoors in a light, cool place. You can keep them indoors as a house plant all year round.

VARIETIES There are numerous species and varieties with different leaf colourations available.

LOCATION Always plant in permeable succulent substrate.

AGAVE

— *Agave varieties*

APPEARANCE Agaves are mostly prickly, rosette-forming succulents with thick fleshy leaves.

CARE Like all succulents, the plant is very easy to care for. Overwinter indoors in a light, warm position.

VARIETIES Sisal Agave (*Agave sisalana*) is compact and blue-green, Foxtail Agave (*A. attenuata*) is a variety without prickles.

LOCATION Plant in impermeable substrate, for example succulent substrate. Plant up larger containers than with other succulents.

AEONIUM

— *Aeonium varieties*

APPEARANCE Aeonium forms green and brown-red decorative rosettes, which remain flat or grow on a small stem. Occasionally blooms after a few years and then dies off.

CARE Apart from infrequent slight dampening, no other care is needed. Overwinter in a light and warm location.

VARIETIES *Aeonium arboretum*, the Tree Leek, is the most common type. The variety 'Atropurpureum' has dark red-brown leaves. The *Aeonium* hybrid 'Kiwi' (see photo) has light green-white leaves.

LOCATION Must be planted in permeable substrate.

VEGETABLES

TOMATO

— *Solanum lycopersicum*

SOWING/PLANTING From March sow on windowsill and plant out in the open from mid-May.

CARE Water generously but do not splash the leaves. Provide overhead shelter to prevent brown rot. Regularly removing small side shoots in the leaf axils (pinching out) encourages the formation of the fruit. Plant up large containers (5 litre +).

VARIETIES 'Tigerella' has striped fruit, 'Phyra' has small fruit, 'Tumbling Tom' is a small variety for pots and hanging baskets.

HARVEST Regularly harvest fruit from July to October.

BELL PEPPER/CHILI PEPPER

— *Capsicum annuum*

SOWING/PLANTING From February sow on the windowsill and plant out from mid-May in the open.

CARE Once the fruit starts forming, water liberally and feed. Plant up in large containers (5 litre +).

VARIETIES 'Naschzipfel' is for small containers, 'Jalapeno' is known as a hot variety with small fruit. 'Bulgarian Carrot' (see photo) has c. 9cm-long yellow fruit.

HARVEST Harvest ripened fruit regularly from July to October.

LETTUCE

— *Lactuca sativa*

SOWING/PLANTING Sow salad leaves and lettuces from February on the windowsill. From April plant or sow directly outside. Mix some sand with the soil.

CARE Inspect regularly for pests such as caterpillars and snails.

VARIETIES An early head lettuce variety is the 'Maikönig', the salad leaves 'Red Salad Bowl' are suitable for harvesting in summer.

HARVEST Depending on variety and date sown, pick from April and May, then continuously through to the autumn. Harvest salad leaves bit by bit.

SPRING ONIONS
— *Allium fistulosum*

SOWING/PLANTING Sow from March onwards directly outdoors. For an extended harvest period sow again four weeks later. The recyclable bottles project on page 38 is a fabulous way to plant spring onions.

CARE Make sure to thin out spring onions growing too closely together so that the remaining ones have enough room to develop.

VARIETIES 'Rossa Lunga di Firenze' has decorative red-violet onions.

HARVEST Possible from May to October, depending on when sown.

RADISHES
— *Raphanus sativus*

SOWING/PLANTING Sow outside from March to September.

CARE Radishes have quite shallow roots so prefer small, wide containers that aren't too deep. For this reason, frequent watering will be required.

VARIETIES 'Rudi' is an early ripening variety. 'Cherry Belle' (see photo) is fast-growing and forms glowing red, thin-skinned radishes with a very mild taste.

HARVEST Possible from April to November, depending on when sown.

ROCKET
— *Eruca sativa*

SOWING/PLANTING Sow outside from March to August. Re-sowing is possible every four weeks for continuous harvesting.

CARE Feed the plants only sparingly. In summer it is best to sow rocket in partial-shade.

VARIETIES 'Toscana' and 'Gracia' are good summer varieties. 'Sweet Oak' is a very bolt-resistant variety with a mild sweet note.

HARVEST Regularly harvest individual leaves from May to November. The leaves grow back again after cutting back to a finger's width above ground.

SPINACH
— *Spinacia oleracea*

SOWING/PLANTING Sow in March and April in fairly deep containers. Autumn sowing from August, however in a vertical garden it is sensible to only harvest young leaves.

CARE Keep the soil really moist. Young leaves can be harvested as salad leaves.

VARIETIES 'Butterfly', 'Tarpy' and 'Red Cardinal' (see photo) are robust and mildew-resistant, 'Verdil' is suitable for autumn sowing.

HARVEST Harvest young leaves for salad or mature leaves as a leaf vegetable from April to June.

CUCUMBER
— *Cucumis sativus*

SOWING/PLANTING Plant young plants directly outside from mid-May. Only place in sufficiently large containers.

CARE Ideal for vertical gardens as cucumbers are best grown trained upwards on a climbing support. Give organic feed regularly. Water extremely well and protect from blazing sun.

VARIETIES 'Tanja' is a long salad cucumber, 'Printo' a small snake cucumber. The 'Silor' variety is a mini cucumber.

HARVEST Harvest regularly from June to September.

COURGETTE
— *Cucurbita pepo subsp. pepo*

SOWING/PLANTING Sow outdoors from April or plant young plants in June. Only use sufficiently large containers.

CARE Feed organic fertiliser regularly. Water extremely well and protect from blazing sun.

VARIETIES 'Cocozelle von Tripolis' has green striped, cudgel-shaped fruit, 'Tondo chiaro di Nizza' has round, light green fruit.

HARVEST You can harvest the small, tasty fruit regularly from July to October.

SWISS CHARD
— *Beta vulgaris subsp. vulgaris*

SOWING/PLANTING Sow directly in March and April or on the windowsill. Plant from April in containers at least 15cm deep.

CARE Feed several times a season.

VARIETIES 'Lukullus' is a tasty chard variety, 'Feurio' is a red-stemmed chard, 'Rhubarb Chard' (see photo) is decoratively red-stemmed and leaf and stems are tasty.

HARVEST Possible from May to November. Harvest individual leaves from outside in, always take only a third so they can grow back.

CARROT
— *Daucus carota subsp. sativus*

SOWING/PLANTING Depending on variety, sow directly outside into humus-rich soil from March to May.

CARE You should thin out the small plants after a few weeks so that the carrots that remain can develop well.

VARIETIES For containers, select varieties that will stay small such as 'Paris Market' (see photo), with orange-coloured, round fruits, and 'Adelaide', which remains finger-wide and relatively short.

HARVEST Possible from May to November, depending on variety.

RUNNER BEANS
— *Phaseolus vulgaris*

SOWING/PLANTING Sow directly outside from May to June. Sowing is best done into the ground or into sufficiently large containers. When doing so, place at a maximum depth of 2cm.

CARE You must provide runner beans with some protection from the wind. After your first harvest, you can feed again in order to encourage further cropping. Water the beans copiously.

VARIETIES The 'Borlotto Lingua Di Fuoco' runner bean has a red pod, 'Blauhilde' (see photo) blue, the 'Maxi' dwarf bean is green.

HARVEST Possible from July to October.

THYME
— *Thymus-Arten*

SOWING/PLANTING Plant from mid-May. Propagation can be done with cuttings or layering.

CARE Thyme needs sandy, permeable substrate and loves dry conditions. Protect in winter, above all from wet conditions.

VARIETIES Caraway Thyme (*Thymus herba-barona*) and Lemon Thyme (*T. pulegioides* 'Aureus', see photo) are very fragrant, Cascade Thyme (*T. longicaulis* ssp. *odoratus*) spills over decoratively, Sand Thyme (*T. serpyllum*) is robust and really winter-hardy.

HARVEST When needed, cut off whole shoots.

PARSLEY
— *Petroselinum crispum*

SOWING/PLANTING Sow or plant directly outside from March to August.

CARE At the beginning water copiously, later occasionally. Parsley is very easy to care for and also visually attractive.

VARIETIES 'Mooskrause' is a beautiful curly leaf parsley, 'Gigante d'Italia' (see photo) is a flat-leafed parsley.

HARVEST Bought potted plants can be harvested all year round. Sown and planted young plants are best from June to November.

SAGE
— *Salvia officinalis*

SOWING/PLANTING Plant outside from March to June. Sage propagates really well with cuttings.

CARE A warm position is advantageous. Do not feed. In winter cover with brushwood. Cutting back in early spring ensures the plants will stay compact.

VARIETIES 'Berggarten' has large green leaves, 'Purpurascens' has red leaves, 'Rotmühle' has white-coloured leaves.

HARVEST You can harvest single leaves on a continuous basis. Leaves are eminently suitable for drying.

CHIVES
—— *Allium schoenoprasum*

SOWING/PLANTING Sow directly outside from March to May. Plant out young plants in April and May.

CARE Chives are a really easy plant for newbie gardeners. Keep the ground moist. Chives can be overwintered on a windowsill.

VARIETIES The 'Miro' variety has fine stalks, 'Elbe' has white flowers.

HARVEST From August to October harvest single fresh stalks or cut off completely close to ground level. Re-grows. Flowering stalks are decorative but not palatable.

SUMMER SAVORY
—— *Satureja hortensis*

SOWING/PLANTING Sow Summer Savory from April on the windowsill, and sow directly outside from mid-May or plant out. Winter Savory can be propagated from cuttings.

CARE Feed and water sparingly. Savory requires a light soil. Prune Winter Savory in spring for new growth.

VARIETIES A distinction is made between annual Summer Savory in the garden and perennial Winter Savory, also known as Mountain Savory.

HARVEST Cut off whole sprigs when needed.

MINT
—— *Mentha varieties*

SOWING/PLANTING Sow outdoors from April. Propagation can easily be done via runners and cuttings. Place in fairly large plant pots, as mints are very prone to spreading.

CARE Use plenty of organic fertiliser.

VARIETIES Peppermint (*Mentha x piperita*) is hot, Moroccan Mint (*M. spicata* 'Marokko' or 'Tashkent', see photo) tends to more sweet-hot, Pineapple Mint (*M. suaveolens* 'Variegata') has decorative white variegated leaves.

HARVEST When needed, cut off fresh shoots and pluck leaves.

NASTURTIUM
Tropaeolum majus

SOWING/PLANTING Sow directly outside from mid-May to June, or on the windowsill from April.

CARE In a sunny position and well-watered, the plants thrive without further effort. They attract aphids, which then means that other plants tend to be spared.

VARIETIES 'Alaska Deep Orange' has orange-coloured flowers, 'Empress of India' orange-red flowers. Colourful seed mixes are widely available.

HARVEST Flowers are edible. Seeds can be used instead of capers.

CURRY PLANT
Helichrysum italicum

SOWING/PLANTING Plant from April. Easy to propagate with cuttings. Plant in permeable substrates.

CARE Water occasionally. Can be overwintered in a sheltered location with brushwood protection. Cut back strongly in early spring to keep the plant compact.

VARIETIES This species hails from the Mediterranean and smells pleasantly of curry. The dwarf curry plant 'Aladin' does not form lasting plants.

HARVEST Cut off entire shoots.

LAVENDER
Lavandula angustifolia

SOWING/PLANTING Plant from mid-May. Can be propagated with cuttings. Plant in permeable substrate.

CARE Water occasionally. Remove flower shoots after flowering. Prune into shape in March, but do not cut into older wood. Can be overwintered outside in a sheltered location protected by brushwood.

VARIETIES 'Hidcote Blue' is the blue-violet classic, 'Grosso' is particularly fragrant.

HARVEST Harvest flowering shoots early so that fragrance and aromas are preserved.

ROSEMARY
—— *Rosmarinus officinalis*

SOWING/PLANTING Plant from mid-May. Can be propagated with cuttings. Plant in permeable substrate.

CARE Feed infrequently and water occasionally. Can be overwintered outside in a sheltered location and protected by brushwood.

VARIETIES 'Arp' is a particularly winter-hardy sort, 'Capri' as a trailing version is ideal for hanging baskets. Rosemary is often planted because of its Mediterranean charm.

HARVEST Harvest whole shoots and hang up to dry or use fresh in the kitchen.

RED-VEINED SORREL
—— *Rumex sanguineus* var. *sanguineus*

SOWING/PLANTING Sow directly outside from April or, if preferred, on the windowsill as early as from February.

CARE Red-veined Sorrel prefers soil that is always slightly damp. Occasionally fertilise the plants. As winter-hardy perennials they die back somewhat, but then shoot up again in spring. Cut off the flowers to avoid strong self-seeding.

VARIETIES Red-veined Sorrel is very decorative.

HARVEST Harvest young leaves and eat as an addition to a salad.

LOVAGE
—— *Levisticum officinale*

SOWING/PLANTING Can be sown from March on the windowsill. From mid-May put young plants outside in well-fertilised substrate.

CARE Water generously. Strong cut-back in the summer ensures fresh growth. Divide plants in the autumn and overwinter in a sheltered location.

VARIETIES Maggi herb is often used as a synonym for lovage, but it's a different plant species.

HARVEST Pick individual leaves or stems as required and use to season soups, stews and broths.

STRAWBERRY
—— *Fragaria × ananassa*

PLANTING Plant Alpine strawberries (or wild strawberries) in April and May, garden strawberries as early as August the previous year. Plant in well-fertilised soil. Strawberries also grow in partial-shade, but the fruit ripens better in sun.

CARE Water generously.

VARIETIES 'Mieze Nova' and 'Mara des Bois' are classic garden strawberries, 'Rügen' is a delicious Alpine strawberry. 'Fraise des Bois' is an Alpine strawberry with white fruit.

HARVEST From June to autumn, depending on variety.

RASPBERRIES
—— *Rubus idaeus*

PLANTING Plant autumn raspberries in September and October, summer raspberries in May in humus-rich earth with leaf compost.

CARE Choose large planters and water liberally. Fertilise annually with compost. Train canes as espalier. After harvesting, prune autumn raspberry canes close to the ground. Remove the old shoots from summer raspberries, they fruit on canes from the previous year.

VARIETIES 'Meeker' and 'Malling Promise' (summer raspberries), 'Himbo-Top' (autumn raspberries).

HARVEST Summer to autumn, depending on variety.

BLACKBERRIES
—— *Rubus fruticosus*

PLANTING Plant from mid-May in humus-rich garden soil, ensure good drainage.

CARE Train shoots as a fan-shaped espalier. Remove canes after the fruit has been harvested in the autumn.

VARIETIES 'Theodor Reimers' has not been beaten for taste, but is very thorny. 'Navaho' has no thorns and is trained vertically on the trellis. 'Loch Ness' has no thorns and is trained semi-upright.

HARVEST From July to September. Only berries that have developed their full colour and that almost fall into your hand are ripe.

KIWI

—— *Actinidia arguta*

PLANTING Plant from mid-May on a tall trellis in a position sheltered from the wind. Mix the soil with bark compost. Loves warmth.

CARE It takes two to three years for the first harvest.

VARIETIES Plant not only male but also female plants. 'Issai' (see photo) is a self-pollinating in part mini kiwi. The Weiki Kiwi is particularly frost-hardy.

HARVEST Mini kiwis ripen on the plant from September. Large fruiting varieties have to be stored to finish ripening after harvesting in October.

GRAPE VINES

—— *Vitis vinifera*

PLANTING Best planted in May. A protected, warm position and a permeable soil mix are ideal.

CARE Cutting back radically in late winter ensures strong new growth and a rich harvest. This also ensures the vine is kept in good shape. Only if planted in large containers will you be sure to have grapes. Winter protection is needed when planted in a tub.

VARIETIES 'Arolanka' is a white, early variety. 'Suffolk Red' (see photo) is a pink-coloured, mid-late variety.

HARVEST From August to September.

POME FRUIT

—— *Malus, Cydonia, Pyrus*

PLANTING Plant in the autumn or early spring in nutrient-rich and permeable soil.

CARE When espaliered, stone fruit is space-saving. However, it takes a few years to establish. Pome fruit trees grow well in a tub.

VARIETIES Espalier fruit: for example, pear (Pyrus communis 'Clapps Liebling', see photo). Pillar fruit: 'Red River' apples.

HARVEST Apples and pears, depending on variety, from summer to autumn. Quinces from October, as soon as you can easily rub off the fuzz.

Resources & further reading

RESOURCES

Forest Garden
forestgarden.co.uk
A manufacturer and distributor of a range of garden timber products, from vertical planters to small greenhouses.

Burgon & Ball
burgonandball.com
With a heritage dating back to 1730, Burgon & Ball supply high-quality gardening accessories, tools and gifts.

Scotscape
scotscape.co.uk
Designs, installs and maintains a range of innovative products to encourage sustainable vertical planting, including living walls, living pillars and living art.

The Royal Horticultural Society
rhs.org.uk
The UK's leading gardening charity. Their website features gardening advice, training and learning opportunities, a garden shop and details on their various gardens and renowned flower shows.

National Trust
nationaltrust.org.uk
Cares for the largest collection of historic gardens and parks in Europe, from kitchen gardens and orchard to parkland and mazes.

The Eden Project
edenproject.com
An educational charity and social enterprise based in Cornwall, where the complex features domed botanical gardens. Their store supplies gardening accessories, garden furniture, seeds and gifts.

Plantlife
plantlife.org.uk
An organisation aiming to restore threatened ecosystems in Britain. They offer volunteering opportunities as well as advice and resources on protecting plants and fungi.

Royal Botanic Gardens, Kew
kew.org
Celebrated garden open to the public. Among other learning resources, their website features their Plants of the World database, information on botanical courses and an online shop.

Botanical Society of Britain and Ireland (BSBI)
bsbi.org
Promotes the study of British and Irish flora, supporting both amateur and expert botanists in researching and recording plants.

FURTHER READING

Fisher, S. (2013). *Growing Up the Wall.* Bloomsbury Publishing, London.
A practical, illustrated guide to growing edible crops using special containers, growing frames, wall boxes, hanging baskets and ladder allotments among other methods.

McTernan, C. (2022). *City Veg.* Bloomsbury Publishing, London.
A season-led, candid guide to growing organic vegetables, herbs and fruit in small urban spaces, with advice about planning, designing, harvesting and cooking with produce.

Angel, H. (2023). *Planting for Pollinators.* Bloomsbury Publishing, London.
An easy-to-use, beautifully illustrated gardening book filled with practical tips on how to encourage insect pollinators into all sorts of gardens – whether a window box, urban balcony or a large garden.

First, J. (2013). *Hot Beds.* Bloomsbury Publishing, London.
Describes the ancient method of growing vegetables in hot beds to garden throughout the year: enabling you to harvest fresh salads in March and potatoes in early April.

Dowding, C. (2019). *How to Create a New Vegetable Garden.* Bloomsbury Publishing, London.
An inspiring step-by-step guide on planning, sowing and growing vegetables, with guidance on polytunnels, greenhouses, no-dig techniques and mulch.

Dowding, C. (2018). *Organic Gardening.* Bloomsbury Publishing, London.
Reveals the art of the no-dig approach to growing delicious organic fruit and vegetables throughout the year using raised beds.

Kullmann F. (2021). *Grow Your Own Mushrooms.* Bloomsbury Publishing, London.
Illustrated with photographs throughout, this lovely guide provides easy-to-understand instructions on how to grow, harvest and preserve the most popular mushroom varieties indoors year-round.

Rook, H. (2022). *Urban Wild.* Bloomsbury Publishing, London.
A practical book filled with seasonal, step-by-step activities to open the door to nature in urban and suburban landscapes, from culinary and herbal projects to mindfulness.

Index

Picture credits

GREEN BOOKS
Bloomsbury Publishing Plc
50 Bedford Square, London, WC1B 3DP, UK
29 Earlsfort Terrace, Dublin 2, Ireland

BLOOMSBURY, GREEN BOOKS and the Green Books logo
are trademarks of Bloomsbury Publishing Plc

First published in 2022 in Germany as *Vertikal Gärtnern* by Franckh-Kosmos Verlags-GmbH & Co. KG
First published in 2023 in the United Kingdom as *Vertical Gardening* by Bloomsbury Publishing
This edition published by arrangement with Franckh-Kosmos
Verlags-GmbH & Co. KG, Stuttgart, Germany

Copyright © Martin Staffler, 2022
Translation © Maureen Millington-Brodie, 2023

A catalogue record for this book is available from the British Library

Library of Congress Cataloguing-in-Publication data has been applied for

ISBN: PB: 978-1-3994-1317-6

2 4 6 8 10 9 7 5 3 1

Layout for this edition by Rod Teasdale
Printed and bound in Austria by Gugler GmbH

To find out more about our authors and books visit www.bloomsbury.com
and sign up for our newsletters